If you were in this world died just for you to reveal the heart of God the father for you His Beloved daughter.

Be Assured of my love + prayers for you,

Blessings + Shalom,

Cindy Burdett

484 802-8982

In Dedication

In Thanksgiving for God's Mercy which drew me

His Love which beckoned me

His Grace which sustained me

And His Passion that filled me

And to the Blessed Mother

Whose unfailing intercession

Guided, protected and transformed me.

And to my Beloved Husband

Whose encouragement and support inspired me

To put the whole account on paper.

Cynthia Jill Smook Burdett

June 3rd, 2009

From Kosher  to Catholic

Memoirs of a Fulfilled Jew
Cynthia Smook Burdett

So, what's a nice Jewish girl like me doing writing a story like this? Sit, we'll talk!

I grew up on Long Island, New York as the youngest daughter of three girls. We considered ourselves to be conservative Reformed Jews. That meant we were pretty serious about our religion and yet somewhat flexible. We attended Synagogue regularly (at least in preparation for all our Bat Mitzvahs and in the Yerzeit* years of beloved deceased relatives), faithfully kept the High Holy Days of Rosh Hashanah and Yom Kippur and we were kosher.

As the daughter of Lawrence and Barbara Smook there were a few basic principles that were just givens:

- you will grow up and go to college,

- you will be Bat Mitzvahed,

- you will never mix milk and meat – unless of course you were in a restaurant, in which case it was kosher not to be kosher,

- and you will never leave the house without lipstick once you were of the age to "need" it.

As Long Island Jews we had a sense of pride in our Jewish identity. We knew we were chosen and somehow set apart from our Christian brethren. We knew that part of being Jewish meant doing mitzvahs for others (good deeds and acts of mercy) and that on Christmas we would probably be going out to dinner or renting a movie. The Holocaust was a painful thread that joined us in solidarity with all Jews. While we had respect and tolerance for other religions (my two best friends were Catholic), my father had recounted how he had been called a Christ killer as a child and how it had wounded him. He taught us more by example than by his words – you'll never be one of them so don't trust them totally.

While other Christian religions were tolerated – the Jews for Jesus were considered anathema by my father. Many a dinner conversation highlighted that it was bad enough to be a "Jesus Freak" but a Jew who claimed to be a believer in Christ was intolerable. According to my Dad being a Jew meant that you didn't believe in Jesus, that you were somehow set apart from all those who did. After all, Jews were the ones persecuted by Christians; they were the victims of the Holocaust, unholy wars and hidden prejudices. The Jews were mistreated and misunderstood. To become a Christian was to become a defector. To claim to be both a Christian and a Jew meant you were playing both sides of the fence and that was reprehensible.

In my household, education was primary. The right to think for yourself and freedom of thought and of religion was sublime. It was the way out of the European ghettos and the way to social advancement. Upward mobility and financial stability were seen as God's blessings. When one was somehow without these there was a hidden feeling that it was God's curse.

I was both Bat Mitzvahed and Confirmed in the Jewish Faith. Confirmation meant that I attended Sunday school until I was 16. I always believed in God in a cosmic and fatherly way but I wondered what happened to all the Old Testament miracles. Why did they seem to die out with the account of the Red Sea parting? I did hear murmurs of miracles from people who claimed to "know Jesus" but I did not plan on getting to "know" Him any time soon.

My two best friends were nominal Catholics and I enjoyed spending Christmas with them but I had a limited understanding of what it meant to be truly Catholic or Christian. My limited understanding was that Catholics had larger families, sent their children to parochial schools if they were "really" religious, did not eat meat on Fridays and for them, premarital sex was taboo. Unfortunately the secular media largely influenced my conceptions with programs like Saturday Night Live which featured "Church Chat with the Church Lady" and the random Catholic School skit highlighting some pent up repressed teen who was forbidden most of life's pleasures by a comical rendition of a knuckle smacking joyless nun. Billy Joel also provided me with an "in depth" understanding of the Catholic Church's teaching on abstinence before marriage by way of his song, "Come out Virginia" wherein he pleads "Don't let me wait – you Catholic girls start much too late. Sooner or later it comes down to fate, I might as well be the one."

So alright already, when did things start to change? Well I entered Al Anon – the 12 Step Program for people directly affected by someone with a drinking problem and that led me to Overeaters Anonymous. Where upon I truly embraced the 12 Steps and began to change my entire life. For those unfamiliar with the 12 Steps, here is a brief synopsis. You admit that you have a problem with some person, place, thing or situation over which you are powerless. You acknowledge that you need help – turn it over to a Higher Power (your own concept of God) and then you begin to inventory yourself to change the things within that you can. You admit your defects/shortcomings to another, get honest, make amends, pray daily and try to give away the healing and good you have received by living this path of recovery.

Living the 12 steps brought me to a deeper conversion. I began to see God – as I understood Him as a God personal to me. A God who cared about me in the now who I could turn to on a daily – if not hourly or minute-by-minute basis. I did not yet truly understand the concept of sin but I sure understood brokenness and dysfunction. Later I came to understand that fallen human nature was at the root of all the dysfunction I had become so acutely aware of. Within the 12 Step programs I found myself drawn over and over again to the Christians. I tried to get more into my Jewishness but always seemed to feel that something or Someone was missing. A popular commercial at the time was Wendy's "Where's the Beef?" and that's what I would ask myself about the attempts I made within Judaism to find a deep personal vibrant spirituality. I was puzzled to consistently find Christians who by calling upon the Name of Jesus seemed to have a light, a hope, a sense of personal commitment and a sense of loving service. The last thing on earth I wanted to do was become a Christian.

I began to pray to God, "If Jesus is really the Messiah, let me know, if he is not, let me know that too because I do not want to offend you." Funny thing, after I prayed that prayer, born-again Christians began to flock to me. I told my friend, Pat, from Al-Anon, thinking she would help me to write off those "crazy Christians!" and wouldn't you know – she was one as well.

I increased my prayer and meditation and began reading just a little of the Bible a friend had given me. I even attended some church services because to me – what I heard in church was a lot like the lifeline I experienced in my 12 Step meetings. At one of the churches – a Nazarene church, they had an altar call. Wherein all who wanted God to live more deeply in their hearts were called to come up. Well I didn't know about this Jesus but I knew that I wanted the one true God to live more deeply within me so I went up . . . and things began to happen.

I stumbled upon a book called <u>Sermon on the Mount</u> by Emmet Fox. It turns out that he is a metaphysician and not a "true Christian" and yet God used his book to have a profound affect on me. Why? Because he started his book by saying, "Who ever you believe Jesus to be – a prophet, a teacher, or the Son of the living God – you cannot deny the truth in the words he taught." That made it safe for me – Miss Long Island Jew to read on. I continued with my prayer and quest to know the truth.

One day I prayed to know that I know that I know what the truth was and became filled with light, peace and love which literally touched my whole body from head to toe. A tingly anointing began at the top of my head until all I could see with my closed eyes was a pulsating light that brought me into peace and love such as I had never known or experienced before. I then heard the words, "Seek and you shall find, knock and the door will be opened."

My fiancée, at the time, knocked on the door as I was having this major spiritual experience and I heard the words, "Do not worry, I will always be with you, I will never leave you." Having been so influenced by Cecil B. Demil's, The Ten Commandments I thought it would be extremely funny if I had turned gray from this experience just like Moses did when he saw God in the movie rendition of what had transpired.

I walked over to the mirror and lifted my hair in the place where the tingles began and sure enough I had an unseemly patch of gray (I was only 22 at the time.) God does have a sense of humor!

I told a woman I knew in the 12 Steps program, about my prayer experience and she invited me to a healing Mass. I had been taking a class in my most secular, unfaithful, party university (Plattsburgh State University in NY) entitled "Evangelism in America." It was taught by an ex-seminarian, divorced Catholic who was bitter about God and the Church. This class was taught during the Jim and Tammy Faye Baker scandal. There were only two people in the class who seemed to believe in God. A guy with the most piercing and peaceful blue eyes I had ever seen, and myself. He loved God and I loved that but he mentioned Jesus all the time and it was annoying. I asked myself and God, "What is that all about?" He had given an oral report about a woman, Janine Nichols, who had the gift of healing. Well, in God's Divine cosmic plan, wouldn't you know that she was the woman who would be praying and talking at this healing Mass my friend had invited me to two years later. Because of all this prior groundwork, I agreed to go with her.

As I sat in the church I was once again anointed by the power of God. I did not yet know that it was the Holy Spirit dancing upon me and Jesus' presence in the Blessed Sacrament, but I did know that I felt peace, love and a presence that I had never felt in any synagogue before. I petitioned God to tell me why. Why did I feel it in church and not in temple?

After the Mass there was time for healing prayer where one could request to be prayed over. There was a huge life size crucifix of Jesus on my right and Janine Nichols stood before me. She sweetly inquired, "What would you like prayer for?" and in my ignorance I said, "I don't know if God wants me to believe in Jesus." As a Jew – it was a sincere cry for the truth. To a Christian it must have sounded absurd. Janine prayed and by God's Divine Wisdom just said, "Don't worry – you will know."

Two weeks later I found myself going on a Charismatic retreat weekend. I went with the idea that I would take what I liked and leave the rest – like we did in the 12 Steps programs. I thought that I was going to take the God stuff and leave Jesus. A woman I met said, "You have such a beautiful devotion to God the Father." I didn't verbalize, "Hey lady, that's the only God I know" but that's what I was thinking.

I planned to go to sleep early to get up in time for the early morning talk that was scheduled but found myself unable to sleep. I did not really have a clue what I was asking for but I found myself begging for Baptism in the Holy Spirit, a greater outpouring of the gifts of the Holy Spirit given at Baptism. The next morning I entered Morning Prayer just a tad late as I had been up all night praying and felt like I was entering into a holy shower. If the Holy Spirit were water I would have been drenched in His love. I felt His power and anointing as my closed eyes witnessed that beautiful pulsating light and I heard the words, "Come, open that last secret door and be baptized in My water and My Spirit." I asked for prayer from the retreat master and as I opened my eyes I saw a statue of the Sacred Heart of Jesus. Statues had always made me a little uncomfortable – as the Jew in me remembered "Thou shall have no graven images before Me." But anointed as I was I said, "O.K. Jesus, Whatever it means to believe in You I'll do."

It's a good thing that God used my "ignorance on fire." It's a good thing too that it was love of Him that drove me. It was all heart. If I had stopped to really contemplate the pain, the hardship and the loss before my heart was captured, I might have missed out on the biggest joy and deepest love my heart has ever known.

After my vow to do whatever believing in Him might require – it was time to put my words into action. Oiy Vey! I had to go home from school for summer break and tell my parents what had happened. I informed them that everything prophesied in the Old Testament about the messiah was fulfilled in Jesus and that I believed in Him. For reformed/conservative Jews who thought themselves to be more enlightened, educated and discerning than the silly old orthodox who embraced myth and erroneous beliefs, the coming of the messiah was seen more as a "messianic age" of peace than of the coming of a particular person.

It didn't matter that every year we would faithfully open the door, set a place and fill a cup of wine for Elijah, the prophet who was promised to return to usher in the coming of the Messiah.

And who knew that the Aficomen we used to hide, (Aficomen, the piece of matzah bread broken off in remembrance of the matzah our forefathers at in haste when they were delivered out of Egyptian bondage, which we wrapped in linen and hid for the children to go and find) was a pre-cursor to Jesus who was born in Bethlehem, which means house of bread, and who would give Himself to us under the form of bread, would be buried in a shroud for 3 days and who the children of Israel were supposed to find, "for unless you become as little children you cannot enter the kingdom of God."

Although we retold the story of Passover every year, we had no idea of the profundity of what God had done. We were taught that the Israelites were told by God to put the blood of a firstborn, unblemished lamb on the doorpost of their house so that the angel of death would pass over the houses of all the faithful Jews and the firstborn sons would be spared. What we never learned was that the reason the Jews at the first Passover were called to sacrifice the lamb at 3:00 and consume it in a meal as opposed to a chicken or any other animal was that lambs were an Egyptian god that the Jews had started to worship as well. God's command was designed to help the Jews separate themselves from their worship of false gods. The blood on the doorpost was also meant to be a sign to the Egyptians that the Jews would no longer be slaves to their gods. When I ponder the significance of the firstborn son, Jesus as the spotless Lamb of God who was slain at 3:00 to save us from our false idols, I marvel at the Father's awesome salvific plan.

Although my family raised their glasses each year at our sedar table in a heartfelt toast to "next year in Jerusalem" in a longing for that messianic peace, no one actually believed that the promise of God was real and that He would indeed fulfill it in a very literal way (and that He had already fulfilled it over 2,000 years ago).

Perhaps in a way, it was their belief in the immensity and awesomeness of an omnipresent, omnipotent God that prevented them from believing that His great love and mercy could cause Him to have such an incarnational redemptive plan.

The Jews were waiting for something bigger, more extravagant. Not the Anointed One riding into town on a donkey, not a bloody crucifixion and certainly not all that poverty, humility and lowliness displayed in the person of Jesus Christ. Somehow my father was sorely disappointed in me for being so foolish and naïve as to accept the "Jesus myth".

At this early stage I was not yet Baptized, Confirmed or even sure of what religion I should embrace. For me the greatest divide initially was between Judaism and Christianity. Accepting Christ was the key that opened the floodgates of Heaven. I began taking Lutheran conversion classes because my friend, Pat, invited me. I should have considered Greek Orthodox because my fiancé at the time, whose name was Christos, was a practicing Greek Orthodox from Cyprus. But I prayed and prayed and God began to reveal profound truths to me. Jesus revealed to me that only the Catholic Church was the true universal family of God, that he intended Israel to be from the beginning, from the call to Abraham – to be the father of many nations and that through him all the nations of the earth would be blessed.

Jesus also revealed to me that only the Catholic Church had belief in His true presence – Body, Blood, soul and Divinity in the Eucharist (I know now that the Eastern Rite churches as well as the Greek Orthodox Church have His true presence as well but at this early stage God dealt simply with my simple mind. At this juncture the churches in the running were Catholic, Lutheran or another Bible believing Holy Spirit, Praise the Lord church.

Somehow I had no problem understanding how a Jewish mother could intercede on my behalf. After all, my own mother very often went before me to prepare the way with my earthly father, so I could clearly see how a perfect mother could soften the way before my heavenly Abba (Daddy).

I was technically still under my parent's roof and needed to be obedient to my Dad, who insisted that I see the family Rabbi. He hoped that Rabbi Stein could un-brainwash me. When I met with the Rabbi I asked in earnest, "Don't the Jewish people believe in callings? Wasn't Moses called to lead the Jews out of Egypt?" I explained that God had a call for me too – to believe in the truth of His salvific plan. The Rabbi assured me that Moses' call was a "much more intellectual process than that" and we parted company. Two weeks later my eldest sister got married and the Rabbi gave a sermon entitled, "Here I am Lord, Isaiah's answer to God's call." It was amazing to see how God had worked on his heart.

My father's heart would need much more work however. He insisted that I see a psychologist. He would pay for it but he would also choose whom I was to see. I agreed. Unbeknownst to him, the person he chose for me was a Catholic, who he paid $100 per week to help me deal with the opposition I encountered with my family living at home that summer. Once again God's sense of humor strikes.

It is amazing to me that I had the courage and grace to choose the Catholic Church because it meant letting go of Christos who I adored. But God had spoken to my heart, "I am taking away Christos to give you the true Christ." My family could have understood a conversion for the sake of marriage. They might not have rejoiced about it but they would have understood. Conversion for the sake of marriage was considered kosher in Jewish circles especially if the conversion was to Judaism in order to raise the children in one faith. They really thought I had gone mad because I chose to convert in pursuit of the Truth and at a great personal cost.

When I had gone on a retreat a well intentioned woman told me that I could receive Holy Communion if I truly believed that Jesus was present in the Eucharist In my limited way, I did believe, so I received...until I was informed that I had to be baptized and confirmed first. I found a church and a priest and told him my story. I asked if I could be baptized and confirmed right away. He informed me that I would have to wait until I went back to college in the Fall, enrolled in RCIA (Rite of Christian Initiation for Adults) and come into the Church at Easter. Well, in my ignorance, I asked him, "Can we just pray?" We did and he opened the Bible to Acts of the Apostles, chapter 10, verse 47, "Can any forbid water for baptizing these people who have received the Holy Spirit just as we have? And he commanded them to be baptized in the name of Jesus Christ." He then set the date for my baptism and confirmation for two weeks later. I was to follow up with my RCIA classes later.

I returned to Plattsburgh to finish my last semester and discerned that I should stay there after graduation. My Long Island Jewish home was not exactly a welcoming environment for the baby Catholic that I was. I remember confrontations with my father in particular that made me quake – "You mean you believe in the Virgin Birth? How can a newborn baby have sin?" his deep threatening voice would pierce my soul. I would cry, stutter and not have the words to articulate the truths my heart knew. I loved my Dad so very much. Deep within the hearts of my Mother and two older sisters was a fervent desire to make him happy and gain his approval. I felt like I had taken a knife to his heart by accepting Christ and yet I had no choice. God chose me and I had to respond but my choice made me the black sheep and family outcast. The only thing that would give me peace when I had fallen under the pain of it all was the Rosary. My Jewish Mother in heaven's recipe – chicken soup for the soul.

I had the opportunity to go to Medjugorje, (Yugoslavia as it was called then). Where the Blessed Mother is said to be appearing. I had heard of countless miracles and healings people had received in connection with the apparitions. I begged to have the courage of my convictions. Although I firmly believed in the Holy Eucharist and the Blessed Mother Mary, I still had some questions about the authority of the Pope and his teachings on contraception and abortion.

I never felt that abortion was right but I did not feel that I had the right to tell another person what to do. As a Jew I was brought up with a high regard for the intellect as a God given gift. We valued the right to question and think for oneself. As a persecuted people we learned to respect diversity and religious freedom because ours had been denied. Unfortunately, these respectable qualities can become a breeding ground for moral relativism when not combined with a firm moral compass and awareness of objective truth. Our American culture has embraced moral relativism because it rejects the idea that a moral code of right and wrong has been written on our hearts by our Creator. He has revealed this code to us in both the Old and New Testaments. Sadly one of the great lies of our day is that the Bible is not the inspired Word of God. God's law written in our hearts has been drowned out by the din of a godless society that denies that there is an objective truth to be known.

If God has never communicated His plan or His will to us then it is up to individuals to figure out for themselves what is right or wrong. Having grown up under this influence I had many questions.

I wanted to understand why the Catholic Church taught against contraception when most other religions permitted it. Did openness to life mean I was destined to become an indiscriminant baby factory? The image in my mind fostered by the culture of death in which I had been immersed featured me, in a bag dress, no makeup, pregnant with my tenth child as I drove around a dilapidated 15 passenger van held together only by the pro-life bumper stickers on the back bumper.

I had met some really "on fire" bible believers who slammed the Church's rituals, laws and observances as pharisaical, man made rules. If the Church was just a man made hierarchical institution then I did not have to obey its teachings. But Christ said to Peter, "you are Peter and on this rock I will build My Church and the powers of death shall not prevail against it" (Matthew 16:18). Well, which church was He referring to? The Catholic Church, the Methodist, the Lutheran, Episcopal or Seventh Day Adventist? Christ spoke of one church. The only church that existed for 2000 years had to be the one true church that Jesus founded.

Well, perhaps the Catholic Church was the church Jesus founded but did She get off track over the years? After all, didn't the Church care about responsible parenthood? Was it responsible to have children before I was ready or able? Why did so many people say She was so wrong on these issues?

I asked myself if the Pope was truly the successor of Peter? Historical fact can date the founding of the Church back to Peter as the first Pope. If Peter was truly the rock upon which Christ built His Church then I had better take pause to hear him out. Christ promised to send him the Holy Spirit to lead him into all truth (John 16:13). He also promised that the gates of death/hell shall not prevail against His Church, that meant that the Church would be prevented from teaching error, for error is not of the Holy Spirit, for He is the spirit of Truth.

In light of this, perhaps our Holy Father had a thing or two (or two hundred million and two) to teach me. Let's start with Humanae Vitae. The Pope said in 1968 that contraception would lead to a pro death mentality, when no one could fathom that it would become legal to abort a baby minutes before natural birth. Who would have foreseen the horrors of partial birth abortion, babies found abandoned in dumpsters and mothers murdering their children? The Pope did! Who would have guessed that we would deal with euthanasia on such a massive scale? Our Holy Papa had the prophetic insight to see what a slippery slope contraception would become.

A quick stroll down the self help aisle of any Barnes and Noble perusing title such as, <u>Men Who Hate Woman and the Women Who Love Them</u>, <u>Smart Women, Foolish Choices</u>, <u>Dealing With Your Non-Committal Man</u>, confirm the Pope's warning that a contraceptive culture would "give cause for alarm is [because] a man who grows accustomed to the use of contraceptive methods may forget the reverence due to a woman, and, disregarding her physical and emotional equilibrium, reduce her to being a mere instrument for the satisfaction of his own desires, no longer considering her as his partner whom he should surround with care and affection" (On the Regulation of Birth, Pope Paul VI, July 25 1968).

I pondered the almost impossible Church teachings on chastity before marriage. I certainly never condoned sleeping around but what about when you find the person you will marry? Perhaps our Holy Father as well as our heavenly Father anticipated just how many "Mr. Rights" would turn out to be "Mr. Wrongs!"

Little by little I began to see the breadth and the depth and the height of wisdom God has given to Holy Mother Church. He has given us a moral compass in a world that lacks one. Following this compass is not always easy. Jesus never promised me a rose garden, a garden of Gethsemane – yes, a rose garden – no. It is a narrow road and worldly wisdom is diametrically opposed to heavenly wisdom.

I praise God for the Catholic understanding that we have been put on this earth to know, love and serve Him. It is also a tremendous gift to know that the purpose of marriage is not only companionship but also a vocation to help your spouse to heaven. Our Holy Mother Church teaches us that self-donative love makes it possible to have truly, holy joyful marriages. Love that dies to self makes it possible to fully live through the storms of life. When properly viewed, openness to life is actually openness to greater blessing. We are actually permitted the honor of becoming co-creators with the Creator. By our yes to God we say yes to one more immortal soul for all eternity. Planned Parenthood never mentioned the immortality of the baby's soul. Humanity at its lowest can be selfish and depraved but raised to its highest, humanity can find true union with the perfect love which is God (the Apostle John says, "let us love one another; for love is of God and he who loves is born of God and knows God…God is love, and he who abides in love abides in God, and God abides in him (1 John 47,16)). The sacrifice required by lovingly raising children is a sure path to sanctity because it is indeed the way of the Cross unto salvation when embraced with our eternal reward in view. To put it into plain English, raising children is just plain hard and requires much death to self. However it is true that in dying we are born to eternal life.

These understandings were the bountiful blossoms I received as a gift in bud form when I went to Medjugorje. I didn't immediately have answers to my questions but I had a "peace that passes all understanding" and knew that the Church did have all the answers. God in His tender mercy would continue to reveal more and more as my soul became ready to receive.

Although I was raised to be a law-abiding citizen I learned that a law that goes against God's law is unjust and need not be followed. I wanted to give voice to the hidden holocaust of abortion. A person very dear to me had had an abortion when I was in High School and I was powerless to help prevent it or to help her at the time. I felt called to join a group called the Lambs of Christ partially in reparation for that abortion and partially to join in sacrificial union with the lambs who fought the war of abortion on the front lines by prayer, educating the public and by blocking entrance to abortion mills. Though, I never intended to be such a maverick, I felt that I needed to tell the world that abortion was murder and not a viable choice. I called my parents from the first prison where I was incarcerated, "Hello, this is Elijah (my jail name) calling collect" . . . . they could have plotzed.

Oiy Vey – a few more gray hairs for the folks and an unintentional twist of the knife in their hearts from the choices I made. I devoted one year to rescue and was in and out of jail, the longest stay was 106 days in North Carolina. We were sentenced to 18 months but were let out early because of overcrowding in the prison. I saw my 27th birthday in a nasty jail-issued gray dress (it did nothing for my figure) overlooking the barbed wire courtyard in the maximum security section in which we were placed because we - the passive, non-violent Lambs - who identified with the helpless unborn child were considered a security threat.

It occurred to me that it was time to return to the real world – I had given over my career and schooling to God like Abraham gave over his son and felt like God was giving it back to me. I felt it was time to blossom where I was planted. I kept hearing the commercial for Snickers, "No matter how you slice it, it comes up peanuts." Translated in my little mind, it meant, no matter what you do – do it for Christ where you are. Be leaven in the work place. I also felt I needed to show my family a balanced, stable and responsible example.

In my biblical studies class at the university, we learned that God created Eve as Adam's most perfect, most suitable partner, his azer kennegdo, who was to be his helpmate and companion. This became my prayer. Very often I know what God is doing in my life by how he inspires me to pray. I kept praying that God would help me not to miss my Azer when he came. Years late I would find out why.

I had always dated guys whose names ended in a vowel. You know, the dark, hot-blooded Italian, Greek or Spanish looking fellows who need some type of conversion or something "fixed", but boy could they dance! When I met my fair complected, holy, kind and gentle German/English husband, my soul was immediately drawn to the beauty of his soul. My heart however wasn't. This turned out to be one of God's greatest blessings. Why? Because I just wanted to be friends with him. There was no date face, no trying to impress him or any dysfunctional, co-dependant "one of us needs to change" dances to attend. In this way, God was able to join our hearts together and then remove the veil. Now truly I see that God's ways are not our ways but Oh how much better they are. And by the way, Paul is also a convert, from Lutheranism, but that's another story.

Things eventually got better with my estranged family. Though they never sat Shiva for me, I always felt that there was many a day they wished they would have.

Although my father refused to give me away if I got married inside a church, he did agree to give me away at a Catholic wedding outside of one. We got a special dispensation to have a Catholic service outside of a church since my side was all Jewish and his was all Lutheran. We proceeded to have one of the most beautiful weddings I have ever seen. Forgive my bias but it was amazing to see how God's grace flooded forth and blessed everyone in attendance with the truth of who He is and the magnitude of what He has done.

Paul and I have been married almost nine years and have three precious children – Tereze Mykiella (7 years old, named after St. Therese the Little Flower and St. Michael) and Noah Lawrence Kolbe (almost 6 years old) and

Moses Joseph Pio (three years old). God has worked a beautiful understanding between my family and me about religion; and my Father is now Catholic. O.K., O.K. My Dad is now Catholic because he passed away and has seen God face to face but seriously, we have a much better relationship now.

We conceived Noah at just the time when my Father was diagnosed with cancer. It was a bittersweet time filled with extraordinary graces. I had the opportunity to spend the last week of my Dad's life with him. While my sisters, who had flown down to Florida (yes, of course, don't all retirees from Long Island go straight to Florida without passing go?) to be with him had left because it appeared he took a turn for the better, I was able to stay. At this point – enter stage left – two holy Catholic nurses who would pray around the clock for my Dad with me. I had forgotten my favorite prayer book but the male nurse let me use his copy. In it was a story called the Three Beautiful Prayers about a Pope who was dying in sin. He told the priest who was praying for him that he surely deserved to go straight to hell in a hand basket. The priest undauntingly persevered in prayer and trusted in God's mercy.

The prayers are as follows:

Lord Jesus Christ! Thou Son of God and Son of the Virgin Mary, God and Man, Thou who in fear sweated blood for us on the Mount of Olives in order to bring peace, and to offer Thy Most Holy Death to God Thy Heavenly Father for the salvation of this dying person... If it be, however, that by his sins he merits eternal damnation, then may it be deflected from him. This, O Eternal Father through Our Lord Jesus Christ, Thy Dear Son, Who liveth and reigneth in union with the Holy Spirit now and forever. Amen

Lord Jesus Christ! Thou Who meekly died on the trunk of the Cross for us, submitting Thy Will completely to Thy Heavenly Father in order to bring peace and to offer Thy most Holy Death to Thy Heavenly Father in order to free...(this person)...and to hide from him what he has earned with his sins; grant this O Eternal Father! Through our Lord Jesus Thy Son, Who liveth and reigneth with Thee in union with the Holy Spirit now and forever. Amen.

Lord Jesus Christ! Thou who remained silent to speak through the mouths of the prophets: I have drawn Thee to me through Eternal Love, which Love drew Thee from Heaven into the body of the Virgin, which Love drew Thee form the body of the Virgin into the valley of this needful world, which Love kept Thee 33 years in this world, and as a sign of Great Love, Thou hast given Thy Holy Body as True Food and Thy Holy Blood as True Drink, as a sign of Great Love, Thou has consented to be condemned to death, and hast consented to die and to be buried and truly risen, and appeared to Thy Holy Mother and al the Holy Apostles, and as a sign of Great Love Thou hast ascended, under Thy own strength and Power, and sitteth at the Right Hand of God Thy Heavenly Father, and Thou has sent Thy Holy Spirit into the hearts of Thy Apostles and the hearts of all who hope and believe in Thee. Through Thy Sign of Eternal Love, open heaven today and take this dying person…and all his sins into the Realm of Thy heavenly Father, that he may reign with Thee now and forever. Amen

My Mom prayed these prayers out loud on her knees at my Dad's bedside – good thing he was in a coma! She also attended Mass with me the Thursday before he died. We had made plans to go to the 5:15 Mass the next day, Friday. If any family member agreed to go to Mass with me you could bet I would make every effort to facilitate it but as I was up all hours from Thursday to Friday I felt the Holy Spirit push me out the door to go to 7 a.m. Mass (for those who know me, attending a 7 a.m. Mass in itself is a miracle). I received Holy Communion for my Dad at 7:24 a.m. When I left the Mass there was a huge rainbow in the sky that lasted about 45 minutes. I knew that I knew that I knew that my Dad had died and that he was O.K. Years earlier my Dad had heart surgery and while praying for him I saw a rainbow. His recovery was nothing short of miraculous. So it truly spoke to my heart when I saw the rainbow after praying for my father. It was a special sign to my heart of God's love, mercy and provision for my Father's soul. When I walked into my Mom's home, she ran to tell me what I already knew – my Dad had died at 7:24 a.m., the exact moment I had received Communion for him.

I decided then that if the child I was carrying in my womb was a boy, I would name him Noah for the rainbow and Lawrence for my Dad. Since I was an AMA (Advanced Maternal Age) when I was pregnant (I was only 35!!!!) I had a 2nd degree sonogram that my doctor scheduled without my knowledge for March 16th – my Dad's birthday. It was then that we found out that the baby was indeed a boy, the first male grandchild in my immediate family. We later came to find out that the name Noah Lawrence actually means Peaceful Rest.

In those three beautiful prayers – after the Pope appears to the interceding priest, the priest asks, "Who will believe the truth about the power of these prayers?" The Pope answers "Go and place them on the altar of the chapel named the Assumption of Mary. Guess when Noah was born – August 15th, the Feast of the Assumption. May our God be praised.

God continues to work on my family. My one sister Dara attended Mass with us on Easter Sunday and said she would be willing to come back again. She also prayed a very dangerous prayer on her knees at St. Patrick's Cathedral a few days later, she had no knowledge of this but it happened to be the day of the Divine Mercy novena where we are asked to pray for those who do not yet know Jesus. Her prayer, "God if Jesus is really the Messiah let me know – if not let me know that too." Which is the very same prayer that I had prayed. Since then she has watched the movie, "Jesus of Nazareth" and has lots of questions. We know she is on good footing because Jesus Himself said, "Seek and you shall find, knock and the door shall be opened" (Matthew 7:7-8).

Personally, I just can't wait to see the "good things of the Lord in the land of the living" (Psalm 27:13).

"So, You Believe in the Virgin Birth??????"

The words of my father still resound in my mind-"You mean you believe in the Virgin birth? Those words packed a powerful punch. First of all, because he said them in a voice not quite his own, way deeper with an eerie kind of pitch. I wasn't sure if I'd soon be seeing green pea soup flying and heads turning 360 degrees like in the 1973 movie "The Exorcist" and; Secondly because his words reflected the betrayal I know that he felt. How could his daughter who was educated at such a great expense (He had worked so hard to send all three of his daughters to college, and to Hebrew and Sunday school. He and my Mom had tried to be faithful examples of good Jewish mensches (that's Yiddish for good-salt-of-the-earth-type people) to give us the proper formation so that we could make educated, well informed decisions about life. His penetrating and sincere big brown eyes searched mine for an answer, "You mean you believe in Original Sin-that a pure innocent little baby is capable of sinning?"

In my fear, in my youth and out of my love for my father who I knew I had hurt terribly I could only answer "I don't know Daddy-I just believe in Jesus."

Then I could only apologize-today by God's grace I am an apologist-that is someone who (attempts) to explain the faith. I would like to offer this talk in memory of my beloved father although he really doesn't need the answers anymore. He has had the beatific vision and is either enjoying Purgatory or Heaven as we speak. However, Christians and Jew's alike do need the answers this side of heaven -St. Paul tells us to be ready to give an account and a reason for the hope that is within us. Why? Because knowing the answers to these questions radically changes our hearts, minds, spirits and souls. When we are transformed into God's image and likeness we can transform the world.

The core questions are,

- What is Original Sin and how did it affect us?

- What was God's Plan for the Salvation of Mankind?

- How is it fulfilled in Jesus Christ?

Original Sin and its effects

Picture this; A beautiful garden, Sunny day, awesome trees- coconuts as big as your head, bananas, grapes, apples, oranges all yours for the picking. Adam, the first man looked at the garden filled with food. He gazed at the cute and tame little lions, tigers and bears (oh my) that he had the privilege of naming and found no suitable partner with whom to share paradise. So God sprinkled a little sleepy dust (I wish I had some of that for my children) and did a little surgery. He removes Adam's rib and from it creates this stunningly beautiful Woman who is to be his most perfect, most suitable partner. (His Azer Kenegdo). Upon seeing this vision of beauty, Adam exclaims "This one, at last is bone of my bone and flesh of my flesh; this one shall be called 'Woman,' for out of 'her man' this one has been taken. In the Book of Genesis (2:24) we find the first marriage-a "Garden Wedding" and this is why a man leaves his father and mother and clings to his wife and the two become one flesh.

Well, before Eve even arrived on the scene God had put Adam in charge. He set him up to cultivate and care for the garden with a few simple rules: You are free to eat from ANY of the trees of the garden except for the tree of the knowledge of good and evil. From that tree you shall not eat; the moment you eat from it you are surely doomed to die". The two of them were quite happy - they ate to their hearts content, they were naked and had no shame or fear of "looking fat" and; they actually got to "walk with God' on a regular basis.

Then enter stage left: Mr. Nigley himself. (That's our family's term for Satan. According to Webster's dictionary to niggle is to pay excessive attention to unimportant details; to criticize and raise difficulties in petty accusations - it's an onomatopoeia-it sounds like what it is-NIGGLE).

So Mr. Slime Bucket himself slithers over to the happy couple to do what he does best-cause fear, worry, and doubt. He asks them "Did God REALLY tell you not to eat from any of the trees in the garden?" The woman spoke up "We may eat of the trees in the garden; it is only about the tree in the middle of the garden that God said you shall not eat it or even touch it she adds (the first embellishment), lest you shall surely die." Nigley replies, "you certainly will not die. Au contraire-God knows that the minute you eat of it your eyes will be opened and you will be like gods who know what is good and what is bad." (Gen3: 3-6)

What a lying dog! It's important to recognize it here because Satan used the same tactics then as he uses now. First, he got Eve to doubt herself and God's command. He twists the truth and projects his evil motives onto God. Satan is the one who wants us all to die. At this early point in the Bible we know that God is the loving Father who created us and who walked among our first parents in the spectacular garden of his own making. Secondly, the old serpent twists the truth and causes confusion. While it is true that their eyes were opened (Gen. 3:7). God himself said, "Behold man has become like one of us knowing good and evil," they became blinded to the true wisdom, knowledge and understanding of God. And while it is true that they did not die physically at that moment, spiritually the life of sanctifying grace in their souls was squelched.

One of the great legacies of the Fall is that now "we see as through a veil" and we have to work to get in communion with God. The truth that Jesus Christ revealed to us is that we are beloved children of a Father who loves us so much "that he sent his only begotten Son that none should perish but shall have eternal life". We will get more in to Jesus as the fulfillment of God's saving plan later but for now - Can you see how Satan uses the projection of his evil intent onto others.

As it was then so to is it now. Was this not evident in the election campaign? Whatever your feelings about President Bush may be in regards to war or economics aside; he has stood up for what we know to be the revealed will of God concerning life. We know from both science (because we can now follow a child's development from conception onward) and religion ("before you were formed in the womb I knew you") that life begins at conception. As such, the other side has been relentless in demonizing Bush. The Kerry campaign made him out to be the candidate who doesn't care for Women's Rights. The liberal media saw Bush as the cowboy who wants to herd up all the women and get back in the kitchen barefoot and pregnant. Their campaigning has been so effective that 12 and 13 year old Catholic girls in Pennsylvania proudly declared that they would vote for Kerry because he would protect their right to choose.

Choose what? There are some choices that are not choices at all because they produce bondage and death. Most women don't "choose" abortion because they see the world as their oyster and have the freedom to do whatever they want. It's never-gee I'll have the lobster, baked potato, oh and the abortion too please. No they make the choice not to have a child because of fear of some sort. Either it is fear of financial trouble, emotional upheaval, suffering or loss. In the garden Adam and Eve "chose" to eat the fruit because they feared death. Satan had cunningly said, "You surely will not die if you eat the fruit" implying that you just may kick the bucket if you don't. Both our first parents then and the woman who "Chooses" abortion today quickly finds out that they have been duped. Abortion is supposed to make the problem go away but instead causes hidden grief, depression, shame and interpersonal problems. The choice of our original parents failed to increase true freedom but instead inaugurated death, shame, darkened intellect, and concupiscence (otherwise known as the weakened will).

What else did Mr. Nigley attack in that garden? It's important to see that in bypassing Adam, who was set in charge by God, and asking Eve "what did He say?" Satan was attacking at God's familial structure. Once you can tear away at the peaceful union between a man and a woman, you can bring disorder and discontent into the family. As it was then so it is now. Satan has attacked at the heart of society, which is marriage. Once you chip away at the foundation it is easy for the fall to follow; and so it did. After the apple luncheon Adam and Eve realized that they were naked and they hid in shame. God asked them why they were hiding and they began the blame session: "the woman whom YOU put here with me - she gave me the fruit so I ate it. God asked Eve "Why did you do such a thing?" She replied "The Serpent tricked me into it, so I ate it."

Being the ultimate good Father that God is - He metes out the punishments - the devil gets to crawl on his belly and eat dirt. Plus God promises to put enmity between Satan and the Woman; "between your offspring and hers; He will strike at your head and you will strike at his heel." This is known as the Protoevangelium-the first Gospel. It is actually the first announcement of the Messiah and Redeemer. It also foretells of a battle between the serpent and the Woman, with the final victory going to one of her descendants.

For Eve and all women to come intensified pains in childbearing were promised (I wonder if PMS is part of the original curse or just a bonus) and Adam is promised to "till the cursed soil by the sweat of his brow."(Gen.3: 19) Before the Fall, work was not a burden but a joyful collaboration with God in "perfecting the visible creation" (Catechism of the Catholic Church-378) after, it's a real headache. Finally, they all got kicked out of the garden and sent to their rooms-East of Eden that is.

Although Old Testament Jews believed in the concept of original sin, (after all it's in their Bible) the ultimate meaning is revealed in the life, death and resurrection of Jesus Christ who comes to us as the New Adam. Basically, man, tempted by the devil stopped trusting in God's goodness and disobeyed. Man was created in holiness and destined to be "divinized" by God in glory instead they went for the cheap imitation wanting to be like god but without God." (CCC-398) They could have had the diamond but instead went for the cubic zirconium.

Marriage became tense and marked by lust (not love), and domination instead of the mutual self-donative affair it was meant to be. God intended for marriage to be an exclusive, indissoluble commitment of life and love entered into by a man and woman for their own good and for the procreation and education of offspring. Did you catch that? God's design for marriage is between a man and a woman. (It was Adam and Eve not Adam and Steve.) That might not be "politically correct" but it is theologically sound. Pope John Paul II says that:

"In this entire world there is not a more perfect, more complete image of God, unity and community. No other human reality corresponds to that Divine mystery so well."

Why then do we see 50-60% divorce rates, pain and difficulty in marriage? Why are Men from Mars and Women from Venus? Why is it so darn hard to get him to share his feelings and for her to just stop nagging him to take out the garbage? It's the result of the fall. But don't you know that "God works all things together for good for those who love him and are called according to his plan (Romans 8:28). God uses this challenge to help us grow in holiness and sanctity. The soap operas don't tell us that the purpose of marriage is to help your spouse to get to heaven and "Cosmopolitan" magazine certainly doesn't mention that dying to our selves through self-donative love is the key to true marital harmony but that's the truth. God had an original intent for marriage and a plan for its execution after the fall. Through Jesus Christ marriage is raised to the level of a sacrament to image the love of Christ for his bride, the church. By the power imbued in the sacrament, itself, man and woman are empowered to love each other with Christ's very own love.

Adam and Eve were called to this kind of sacrificial love but missed the mark, (the definition of sin is actually to miss the mark). If Adam had protected Eve and the Garden against the threats of Satan he might have indeed been killed but God would have raised him up. Instead, he let fear control him and the rest is history. Now we inherit more than a love of apples and a genetic propensity for fig leaf cover-ups, we inherit all the repercussions of the fall - wounded human nature.

So that is how the harmony within the created world was broken and death enters the picture. The sins of the parents are passed along with genetic features like high cheekbones or brown hair. But God in his infinite love for us had a plan.

When Papa Smook asked me if a little baby was capable of sin what I should have explained were the words of a follower of the famous first century Rabbi Gamliel, we know this follower as St. Paul, who writes in Romans 5:12, 19

"By one man's sin all were made sinners. Sin came into the world through one man and death through sin, and death spread to all men…Then as one man's trespass led to condemnation for all men, so one man's act of righteousness leads to acquittal and life for all men."

Jesus is the New Adam because he became obedient even unto death for the sake of his bride, the one who was disobedient. Mary becomes the new Eve because when she was told about God's redemptive plan she responded "Yes, be it done to me according to thy word". Eve on the other hand responded to God' orders by saying "Never mind your warning, I think I'll have the fruit after all."

God's Salvific Plan

The Bible is God's love letter to us in which he gradually reveals Himself. God has been reaching out to us from the beginning. It's important to realize that Old Testament is not just the history of the Jews but that because of Christ it's all in the family. We are all spiritually Semites. (Mishbukah)

God mapped out his salvific plan even in the first book of the bible, in Genesis. Our mission, should we choose to accept it; is to see just how He did it. God is the loving Father who seeks us out time and time again. Though Adam and Eve were relegated to what seemed like an eternal time-out, God had a plan to turn it all around. He said that "the Woman would crush the head of Satan and her offspring would defeat him." Just what was he thinking?

Well, first He had to enter into a covenant with a people he could call His own. (To enter into a covenant means to swear by oath, which would yield the fruit of blessing or curse.) God was hoping to go heavy on the blessing, light on the cursing. He entered into the Covenant to marry us, "As a young man marries a virgin so your God will marry you," because He loves us and wants to restore the communion we had in the garden and go beyond it to a supernatural level - He chose Abram, a righteous nomad, to be the father of all nations to set the wheels in motion. He called Abram saying, "Have I got a deal for you;"

"I will make of you a great nation, a great dynasty and bless the entire world through your seed." Abram responded, "Sounds good to me. The Lord replied, "O.K. I will call you Abraham but there's just this one thing …I want to mark this covenant with you in your flesh." Abram responds, "Yes, my Lord, sounds great. But, WWWhat's circumcision?"

One thing to get straight about God right now is that His timetable is not ours. The psalmist knew "a thousand years in your eyes are merely as yesterday," He is faithful but sometimes He is slow, at least to our way of thinking, especially to us who are products of McDonald's drivethru's and microwave ovens. Abraham was waiting for the son who was going to bless all the world for so long that when an angel came to visit (Yes, they still made house calls) to say that Sarah would give him a child at the ripe old age of 90, and he was 100, they both just cracked up. So much so that the son who actually did come as promised was named Isaac, which means laughter.

I think Isaac must have laughed nervously after the one day when he was out having "special time" with Dad. He and his father had gone to Mount Moriah to offer a sacrifice to God. Isaac asked in earnest "Where is the sacrifice Dad? Did we forget the lamb?" Abraham responds with, "No my son, Yahweh Jirah-God himself, will provide the sacrifice." Then the next thing he knew his father was binding him up and placing him on the altar. "Uhhh, Dad this isn't funny." Then they heard a voice from heaven say "do not lay your hands on the boy; Because you did not withhold your only son from me, I swear by Myself that I will bless you abundantly and make your descendants as countless as the stars." God swears by Himself to be put under a curse if He does not fulfill His part of the covenant. He wanted to show that He would do whatever it takes to bless us.

After years of therapy, Isaac grows up and has 12 sons who become the fathers of the 12 tribes of Israel. The second to last son, Joseph, was by far Isaac's favorite. He gave him a beautiful multicolor robe (the dye was a hot commodity back then). This incited much envy and resentment from the other sons. Joseph had a gift for dreaming. One morning he awoke to share one of his dreams with his brothers. It went something like this. They were out in the field binding sheaves when suddenly Joseph's sheave stood upright and the brother's sheaves formed a circle around Joseph's and bowed down to his. Not the wisest dream to share with his jealous brothers. Upon hearing the dream they asked "Are you really going to make yourself King over us?" "No, I was just sharing really," he replied. Then he proceeded to share another dream in which "the sun, the moon and 11 stars were bowing down to him." The brothers all thought that Joseph had a real ego problem and needed to be put in his place...far, far away. They sold him into slavery in Egypt.

Joseph languished in jail for a while but God was busy working all things together for good. He used the same gift of dreaming that got him in captivity to get him out. Joseph successfully interpreted dreams for the Pharaoh and was made the Prime minister. He developed an awesome plan to save the people from famine. It's a good thing because all the Jews from Canaan needed his help. Wouldn't you know Joseph's brothers all end up bowing down to him after all.

Fast forward a little bit, the Jewish people are oppressed in slavery, in Egypt, 430 years after Joseph (and God) rescued his brothers from famine in Canaan. But God had a plan. He sends Moses, the Hebrew born-Egyptian prince turned renegade, turned shepherd to bring His people out of Egypt.

God has a passion for choosing the unlikely, unwilling and ill equipped to do His bidding, to show His omnipotent power. Moses had a speech impediment, was a deposed Egyptian prince and wondered how he would ever get the people to heed his words. God said never fear, "It is I who will speak through you and teach you what you are to say...take this staff in your hand; with it you are to perform miracles."(Exodus 4:12) He commands Moses to "perform before Pharaoh all the miracles I will put in your power, I will make him obstinate, however, so that he will not let the people go." (Moses is thinking oiy vey - how am I going to explain that to the people?) Then say to Pharaoh, "Thus says the Lord; Israel is my first- born. Hence I tell you; Let My son go, that he may serve Me. If you refuse to let him go, I warn you, I will kill your son, your first born."

Doing God's work may be blessed but it's never easy. Moses finally got the Jews to trust that Yahweh was really using him to set them free from Egyptian bondage and then after he has his little talk with Pharaoh, Pharaoh says to the Jewish slaves-"Now you can get your own straw for brick-making and I'm increasing your quota." Thanks a lot Moses!

So Moses goes to the Lord and says" Why do you treat this people so badly? And why did you send me on such a mission? Ever since I went to Pharaoh to speak in Your Name, he has mal-treated this people of Yours and You have done nothing to rescue them."(Exodus 5:22)

The Lord answered Moses, "Now you will see what I will do to Pharaoh. Forced by My mighty hand he will send them away...I will take you as My people and I shall be your God." God then sent 10 plagues-Water turned to blood, frogs, gnats, flies, pestilence, boils, hail, locusts, darkness and finally the piesta resistance - God smote the first born of every Egyptian so that Pharaoh's heart would change and he would "let the Jewish people go." He gave Moses some very special instructions for the new holiday He instituted called "Passover" or "Pesach" in Hebrew (which would have significance for all eternity.)

The Jews were instructed to prepare an unblemished lamb, which would be killed in the sixth hour, sprinkle the blood of the lamb on the doorposts using a hyssop branch and then they were to consume the roasted lamb at the celebratory Passover dinner table. From that night onward the Jews were commanded to rejoice and remember what God had done in passing over the firstborn children of the promise when He set them free from Egyptian bondage. His real plan is to free them (and us) from the bondage of sin. We'll look at the fulfillment later.

As a child I loved Passover. Since I was the youngest in the family I had the priviledge of asking the four questions. Manish tanah hal-lie-la haz-eh me-call hal-ley-lote: why is this night different from all other nights? Why on this night do we eat only unleavened bread? Why on this night do we eat especially bitter herbs? Why on this night do we dip the herbs in salt water and charoses? Why on this night do we hold this Passover service? We did so because God commanded it. What a wise Father we have, to require us recount what He did for us each year. He knew that unless we made a conscious effort to recount what He did for us, the story of our deliverance, we might get a bad case of spiritual amnesia and let that "what-have-you-done-for-me-lately-creep-in." After all that tarrying in the hot desert sun, God knew it was important that we keep that "attitude of gratitude." His Word reveals that "God inhabits the praises of his people." So we used to sing a song at the sedar table called Dayenu which means "it would have been enough." Had He divided the Red

Sea and not permitted us to cross on dry land; dayenu. Had He permitted us to cross and not destroy our oppressors; dayenu….Had He given us the law and not led us into the Promised Land. In every generation we were taught to look upon ourselves as if we had personally come out of Egypt because it was for all that God delivered us.

To make a long story short, after a little praisin and alot of kvetching and moaning (but who could blame them - 40 years eating manna and quail in the dusty, hot desert) the Jews finally made it to the land flowing with milk and honey.

Now they wanted a king so God acquiesced, in order, to build an earthly model of His heavenly throne and temple. Who would He choose? After a failed attempt with a previous candidate for the kingship, God chose another unlikely candidate, a young shepherd boy who was extremely good with a sling shot, a man after God's own heart. You may recognize him as the author of many a poetic psalm.

God anointed David as king. One of the first things King David did was consolidate his hold on the Promised Land. You might say that he was in the right war (with the Jebusites –at the right place (Jerusalem) at the right time (when the timing is God's it has got to be right).   He saw himself as a priest-king and offered a sacrifice when bringing the Ark of the Covenant back to his newly won capital, Jerusalem, formerly known as Salem.   It isn't just any sacrifice that will do. David's predecessor Saul had offered similar sacrifices to God before a battle and lost his kingship because of it. The problem was that Saul didn't follow directions very well. The Mosaic Law was explicit in detailing who could act as a priest. Ever since the Israelites fell into pagan worship of the of the golden calf on their desert journey only Levitical priests could offer sacrifice. Before the golden calf, any first-born son of Israel could offer sacrifice. But David saw himself as a priest king in Jerusalem, even going so far as wearing the garb of a Levitical priest. King David blessed the people in God's name and gave them bread, meat (which some scholars translate as wine) and raisin cakes. David had a vision of what God had in mind for all Israelites, that is to be first born, royal, high priests fit to offer sacrifice pleasing to the heart of God. The last priest-king of Salem to do so was Melchizedek, who offered a sacrifice of bread and wine to God and blessed Abraham for his victory in battle.

Jerusalem, the place of the temple means, "God will provide peace." When David had subdued all the area round about Jerusalem and was given rest from all his enemies, he desired to fulfill the commandment of Moses to build a central sanctuary after a full conquest of the Promised Land. But David's heart's desire to build a temple for the Lord was denied to him because of his sin with Bathsheba. This great honor was instead bestowed upon his son, Solomon.

God promised David that instead of David building God a house, God would build David a house, a dynasty that would last into the ages, his son would sit on the throne of David forever; "When your days are fulfilled and you lie down with your fathers, I will raise up your offspring after you, who shall come forth from your body, and I will establish his kingdom. He shall build a house for my Name, and I will establish the throne of his kingdom forever. I will be his father, and he shall be my son." (2 Samuel 7:12-14)

King David's son, Solomon built the temple of the Lord in Jerusalem, but after that, despite all his wisdom, he turned his heart away from God to follow the strange gods of his foreign wives. David's descendants after Solomon went from bad to worse. Finally the kingship was ended in the reign of Zedekiah, and the descendants of King David went into hiding (2nd Kings 25). But what of the promise of God that a descendant of David will sit upon his throne forever. How is God going to work it all out?

God's Plan Fulfilled in Jesus

Fast forward to an obscure town in Galilee called Nazareth. God sent His angel; Gabriel to a virgin (named Mary) betrothed to a man named Joseph, of the house of our buddy, King David. The angel said, "Hail Full of Grace! The Lord is with you…. Behold, you will conceive in your womb and bear a son, and you shall name him Jesus. He will be great and the Lord God will give him the throne of his father David, and he will rule over the house of Jacob forever, and of his kingdom there will be no end. "(Luke 1:26-33)

Mary responded, "How can this be since I have no relations with a man? The angel replied, "The Holy Spirit will come upon you and overshadow you. Therefore the child to be born will be called holy, the Son of God."

The Blessed Mother had alot to ponder. She would have known the scriptures, what we now call the Old Testament by heart, in it she would have read about the long awaited Messiah. She would have known that he was to be - Born of a virgin, a descendant of Abraham, of the tribe of Judah and the house of David. That he would be called into the Lord's service from the womb and anointed by the Holy Spirit and would be born in Bethlehem and afterwards taken into Egypt. She would have known from her pondering of the Word of God that the Messiah would be heralded by the messenger of the Lord, would perform miracles, that the lame would walk, the blind would see, that he would minister in Galilee and preach the good news of God's kingdom. She would have believed that God's Messiah would cleanse the Temple, and that he would enter that City of David as a king on a donkey. She would have known that he would be rejected by the Jews, the very ones he had come to save, that he would die a humiliating death, involving rejection, being betrayed by a friend and sold for 30 pieces of silver, all the while being silent like a lamb led to the slaughter. That he would be mocked, beaten, spat upon, and that they would cast lots for his garments. She would have seen the shadow of the cross, even in Bethlehem; that they would pierce His hands and feet, that he would be crucified with thieves, and even then, he would pray for His persecutors. In the end, they would pierce His side but not break his bones, and bury him in a rich man's tomb. But through it all she would have also known that he would rise from the dead and ascend into heaven to sit at the right hand of His Father.

If Mary had known all these things about the Messiah, why didn't ALL the Jews get it? Why, if he had been prophesized from the beginning of time do our Jewish brothers and sisters have such a hard time accepting him? According to Jewish understanding the Moshiach will be a very righteous man from the family of King David with a total commitment to the Torah. He will be anointed as king of the Jewish people. He will re-establish the dynasty of King David, rebuild the Holy temple in Jerusalem and gather together all Jews from throughout the world to properly observe God's law. He will perfect the world, leading all to serve Hashem (The Holy Name) in Unity. The world will be completely at peace. The Jews were looking at the Messiah from a worldly perspective. They expected a rich king; Jesus was born in a stable. They were looking for world peace, instead he brought peace within. They expected the temple to be rebuilt on earth. Jesus passed judgment upon the earthly temple and promised to rebuild it in three days," referring to His Body the true temple and it's resurrection. The Jews were looking for a re-establishment of David's dynasty; Jesus restores mankind to royal and priestly relationship with the Father lost in the garden and in the wilderness of Mt. Sinai. The Jews wanted freedom from their earthly oppressors. God wanted to free them from the oppression of sin, error and death.

Ultimately, faith is a gift and " the realization of what is hoped for and evidence of things not seen" and requires an assent of the will in humility asking to see with God's vision. Even the disciples who had spent three years with Jesus needed the scriptures opened up to them for the eyes of faith to see (Luke 24:13-35)

It takes the eyes of faith to see that Jesus Christ, Son of Abraham, Son of David, came to bring healing to a broken world, one that was at war with God and God's law, bringing the peace of a renewed relationship between God and his wayward children. God, the Father provides the sacrifice Himself, His very own Beloved Son. From the very same place that Abraham was stopped from offering up his only beloved son, in the fullness of time, God provides His Son to carry the wood for the sacrifice, in the shape of a cross, which is laid upon His scourged back. He takes the curse for our sins upon himself so that we might receive the eternal blessing. "Cursed is he who hangs upon a tree." (Dueteronomy) As the sacrificial Lamb of God, offering Himself on the same mountain range of Mount Moriah, (Calvary is a foothill of that mountain range) He laid down His life for His bride the Church, purchasing her at a great price, every last drop of His precious Blood and crucified Body. He now becomes present to her in the consecration of His Body and Blood on her altars and dwells within her in Eucharistic Communion. Christ, the New Adam gives himself up for His bride and God raises Him up on high, to sit in kingly splendor at His right hand forever on the throne of His father David. Christ, the new Moses, brings His people out of slavery to sin, out of the bonds of the devil and into the Promised Land, the eternal homeland of His Father. Christ, true God and true Man brings our humanity into the very inner life of the Holy Trinity, making Adam's sin into a happy fault that won for us so great a redeemer and so great a redemption.

God Bless this Mess-Finding the Hidden Holiness in Everyday Life

I just read an article that said it's actually good for children to grow up with a little germs and dust because they'll develop stronger antibodies that way. Well, my children are developing the immune systems of Hercules. It's not that I WILL to be such a "relaxed housekeeper," I just can't get a grip on the laundry which breeds in the laundry baskets that never gets put away. I earnestly desire that all my socks would remain happily married to their mates of origin and I fervently desire to weed through my closet for the next St. Vincent DePaul's clothing drive. Somehow, I just can never make it happen. I know that my role as heart of my house is a dignified and respectful one. I want to bring up my children in holiness and peace. It's important that they say their prayers, get plenty of rest, eat their vegetables, and brush their teeth. They should be well fed before Mass so they're not spilling cheerios all over the freshly vacuumed church carpet during the consecration. I realize that I should set out their clothes the night before so that we don't experience Mayhem when even St. Anthony can't locate the lost loafers, and yet, try as I may to get out the door on time with peace, joy and everyone's sippy cup, I find myself invariably dealing with the unexpected poopy diaper that throws the whole universe off kilter. But, "what I do, I do not understand. For I do not do what I want, but I do what I hate: for I do not do the good I want, but I do the evil I do not want to do. "(Romans7: 15-25). In every way, God reveals to me my weaknesses that he may be revealed as my strength. God chose the foolish of the world to shame the wise, and God chose the weak of the world to shame the strong, and God chose the lowly of the world who count for nothing, to reduce to nothing, those who are something, so that no human being might boast before God (1 Cor.1: 27).

I always thought that if I just did my part in life, tried my hardest, gave it the ole Smook college try that things would go well. After all, didn't' God say, "I set before you here this day a blessing and a curse; a blessing if you obey the commandments of the Lord and a curse if you don't?"(Deut.11: 26) I've learned that in God's academy for the purification of souls, things often look their worst when God is doing His best.

Who says miracles aren't still happening today? We witness the miraculous multiplication of clutter in our small townhouse on a regular basis. Having no basement or garage provides a daily opportunity for heartfelt prayer -

"Jesus mercy; Mary help." And; I have the awesome privilege of possessing both Jewish and Catholic guilt. My mother, who was Immaculate from her conception (Not to be confused with the Blessed Mother, who is the Immaculate Conception) is from the school of "If you just clean the shower doors every time you get out of the shower you'll never have to deal with that nasty buildup." She has an invisible holster belt to hold the Windex and paper towels that she draws out automatically (spritz, spritz) after every smudge, drop or drizzle. So when my house gets out of control, so does my mind. Instead of it just being an issue of making some slight revisions in my life to facilitate a change (i.e. just tackle a little a little laundry at a time) it becomes a moral issue in my mind as if I am the sum total of the dusty night stand.

What does all this have to do with Holiness? Everything. It's the day in, day out, awful and awesome, stupid and stupendous things in our lives that God uses to perfect us. In the words of Father Corapi "We are all called to be great saints," "So strengthen your drooping hands and your weak knees" (Hebrews 12:12) and get ready to strike your prayer card pose-one day the Vatican may need it for your cause.

Did you ever have one of those drunken moments with the Lord? I don't mean after consuming a bottle of Chardonnay by yourself...I mean one of those times where you truly give yourself; heart, mind, body and soul to God. You're loving Him so much and you're palpably feeling just how much He loves you too. It goes something like this:

"Yes Lord, whatever you want me to do I will do. Wherever you send me I will go. I surrender all to you. Yes Lord, please make me a Saint. Oh and Lord, I want to be with you right away in Heaven so I'll just do my purgatory on earth and I'll offer you all my prayers, works, joys and sufferings for the salvation of souls, for my sins and the sins of the whole world."

Then you wake up the next morning, still a little hung over, "to smell the coffee" that spilled all over the floor when you were trying to clean up the eggs that your two year old played catch with in the kitchen. Blessed be Jesus, thank you for everything you pray through gritted teeth as you discover that your computer is down and the cell phone you were going to use to call your important client at 2pm just died. Never fear, you can go to a pay phone, except that you have no money till payday..."Uhh, Jesus...about last night."

There is a reading I would like to share with you from my tattered and torn Streams In the Desert devotional, which has carried me through many a peak and valley in my walk with God:

"God forbid that I should glory, save in the cross of our Lord Jesus Christ, by whom the world is crucified unto me and I unto the world (Gal. 6:14).

They were living to themselves; self with its hopes, and promises and dreams, still had a hold of them; but the Lord began to fulfill their prayers. They had asked for contrition, and had surrendered it to be given them at any cost, and he sent them sorrow; they had asked for purity, and He sent them thrilling anguish; they had asked to be meek, and He had broken their hearts; they had asked to be dead to the world, and he slew all their living hopes; they had asked to be made like unto Him, and He placed them in the furnace, sitting by "as a refiner and purifier of silver,' until they could reflect His image; they had asked to lay hold of the cross, and when He had reached it out to them it lacerated their hands.

They had asked they knew not what, nor how, but he had taken them at their word, and granted them all their petitions. They were hardly willing to follow Him so far, or to draw so nigh to Him. They had upon them an awe and a fear, as Jacob at bethel, or Eliphaz in the night visions, or as the apostles when they thought they had seen a spirit, and knew not that it was Jesus. They could almost pray Him to depart from them, or to hide His awfulness. They found it easier to obey than to suffer, to do than to give up, to bear the cross than to hang upon it. But they cannot go back, for they have come to near to the unseen cross, and its virtues have pierced too deeply within them. He is fulfilling to them His promise, "And I, if I be lifted up from the earth, will draw all men unto me."(John 12:32)

But now at last their turn has come. Before, they had only heard of the mystery, but now they feel it. He has fastened on them His look of love, as He did on Mary and Peter, and they can but choose to follow.

Little by little, from time to time, by flitting gleams, the mystery of His cross shines out upon them. They behold Him lifted up, they gaze on the glory which rays from the wounds of His holy passion; and as they gaze they advance, and are changed into His likeness, and His name shines out through them, for He dwells in them. They live alone with Him above, in unspeakable fellowship; willing to lack what others own (and what they might have had), and to be unlike all, so that they are only like Him.

Such are they in all ages, 'who follow the lamb whithersoever he goeth."

Had they chosen for themselves, or their friends chosen for them, they would have chosen otherwise. They would have been brighter here, but less glorious in His kingdom. They would have had Lot's portion, not Abraham's. If they had halted anywhere-if God had taken off His hand and let them stray back - what would they not have lost? What forfeits in the resurrection?

But He stayed them up, even against themselves. Many a time their foot had well nigh slipped; but He in mercy held them up. Now, even in this life, they know that all he did was done well. It was good to suffer here, that they might reign hereafter; to bear the cross below, for they shall wear the crown above; and not their will but his was done on them and in them. Anonymous

If "Jesus, Son though He was learned obedience through what He suffered." How much more do we need to learn the lesson at the College of the Cross. No servant is greater than his master. We are given an awesome and wonderful opportunity to "make up for what is lacking in the suffering of the body of Christ"(Col. 1:24) But what does that mean? Wasn't Christ's offering perfect and lacking nothing. Yes, it was; but He gives us the opportunity to share in His redemptive plan out of love. When I am making a cake I don't really need my daughter to help but out of love I allow her to participate.

The world does not appreciate suffering and will do whatever is necessary to avoid it. Euthanasia, abortion, and contraception are the fruit of the culture of death in which we live, wherein the great mortal sins are inconvenience and right wing conservatism. God forbid that our lives should be altered by an unwanted pregnancy, physical illness or financial set-back. We avoid the cross at all cost.

We divorce because were "incompatible," get Prozac when we're slightly bothered and put our high energy little boys on Ritalin. (I am not saying that there is never a cause for medical treatments when necessary-what I am referring to here is the excessive use of treatments that stem from our excessive avoidance of suffering.)

When my father was dying of cancer, my eldest sister, who was voted "Lawyer of the Year", and I were discussing what would happen if my father had to be put on life support. She was quite adamant that he had "the right to die". I don't question the authenticity of her compassionate outcry for his rights but it was rooted in an erroneous belief system. The "right to life" is based on the fact that life is a gift that we do not possess as a piece of property but as an inviolable right. It cannot be taken away by another person or by the person himself. The "right to die" however, is based on the idea that life is a "thing we possess" and may discard when it no longer meets our satisfaction. The "right to die" philosophy says that there is such a thing as a "life not worth living". Sahbra was sure that my father would not want to live that way. She was absolutely right. He would not have. However, it was not his decision or ours to make. ("Euthanasia & Assisted Suicide" by Father Frank Pavone-the Five Issues that Matter the Most-2004)

Pope John Paul II is an outstanding example of leading from the cross. The news media would like to paint the picture of his tragic suffering and spent pontificate. Why doesn't he just hang up his ecclesial towel and call it a 'ding dong day'?

Why does God allow his beloved servants to suffer so much? St. Teresa of Avila said, "If this is the way you treat your friends...no wonder you have so few." It is precisely because He loves us, that He allows us to "carry around in our bodies the dying of Christ," that we might also more fully share in His glorious resurrection.

When I was pregnant with our third child, our finances were an abysmal mess. Paul was working in a ministry type job and we could barely pay the rent. My sister Dara-the voice of Today's America-told me in no uncertain terms that I was being absolutely selfish to have another child when I couldn't afford the time or the money to care for him. I was doing a dis-service to my other two children and robbing them of what little spiritual, emotional and financial resources we had. She informed me that it wasn't God's will but mine that caused me to "choose" life. And; she added, "if we ever went on vacation and wanted to stay in one room that third child would make it impossible." What she and society overlook is the infinite value of the eternal soul of a child. Mother Teresa said, "It is a great tragedy that one must die that one might live the way they want."

Make no mistake. We are in a battle-our struggle is not with flesh and blood but with Principalities, with Powers, with the world rulers of this present darkness, with the evil spirits in the heavens. Mr. Nigley (that is the devil, Satan, the ole slime bucket himself) wants you more than Uncle Sam. President Bush may not be instituting the draft but Mr. Nigley sure is. The battleground is in the heart of our homes. He's striking at marriage and family because both were designed to image and reflect the heart of Christ. God in His eternal wisdom knew that if there was anything this side of heaven to draw us out of our selfishness; it is a spouse with a different opinion and children with unlimited demands. The world, the flesh and the devil tell us that the grass is greener somewhere else. That life should be easy, that our spouse should make us happy and that our cupboards should be full.

The truth is that marriage is a call to ongoing conversion with the cross at the center. God never promised us a rose garden; a garden of Gethsemane, yes; a rose garden, no. We are called to help our spouse to heaven. Doesn't that truth just set you free? Our mission, should we choose to accept it, is to help our beloved to the pearly gates. When marriage becomes all about what we "feel" and how "fulfilled" we are; we are heading down that slippery slope to the 50-60 percent divorce rate.

According to Christopher West who echoes John Paul II thinking on the Theology of the Body:

"Marriage is the intimate exclusive, indissoluble communion of life and love entered by a man and a woman at the design of the creator for their own good and the procreation and education of children. It calls for mutual self-surrender. In marriage, we become one in body and soul. That is why the Church doesn't so much teach that divorce is wrong, but that it is impossible."

It is impossible to fulfill our mission on earth without suffering. In a sense, it is easier to suffer when it is some big blatant trial, where you have obviously no place else to go but into the arms of Jesus. But so often, it's the absolutely hidden interior struggles that only you and Jesus know about. Saint Therese, the Little Flower knew this interior suffering all too well. In fact, so hidden was she, that when she died, the sisters in the convent were concerned that they would not have enough material for her obituary. Today, she is a Doctor of the Church whose doctrine of the 'little way" has transformed millions of lives. A great cross is very often the prelude to a great grace. Suffering ripens the soul to receive God's love.

We have all heard the story of Job. He was a good and faithful man. He walked uprightly and loved God. He had been extremely blessed with wealth and a happy family life, until one day when our Lord had a conversation with the old serpent himself. Mr. Nigley asked for permission to test Job saying that He only believed in God because he had been so blessed. As things started to go from bad to worse in Job's life, his friends began to question what he had done wrong to deserve such misfortune. Isn't that what happens in our lives as well?

Before I became a Christian I had the grand illusion that I was in control. If I wanted to achieve some lofty goal I could achieve it with fortitude, faith and perseverance. I had struggled with weight issues from the time I got my tonsils out when I was 5, so by the time I hit 18, I was ready to gain control. I joined a 12-step program to deal with my "food issues." Though I had given it over to God as I understood him; I didn't understand him well enough. For three years I weighed and measured every meal, ate nothing in between and exercised religiously everyday. As a result I was very fit but was held captive by my obsession with weight control. In my control, I was a slave. In the eyes of my family I was doing great, because you know - "It is better to look good than to feel good." Then I became a Christian. I gave Jesus my heart and my will and begged Him to heal me. He said O.K. but hold on for the ride. Things could not have looked worse. God started to heal me of the shame monster that was the root of my woundedness and I began to get more normal with food. In the process I gained weight. I had just told my family that I believed in Jesus and was at a diner with my sister Dara. There was a homeless preacher with long hair and no teeth on the corner saying "Repent and Believe!" I didn't look that good because nothing fit and my sister looked out the window at the street preacher and said "Is that your aspiration?"

It appeared that I was falling apart. In a sense I was. God's grace was at work within me. As St. Paul says: "We hold this treasure in earthen vessels, that the surpassing power may be of God and not from us. We are afflicted in every way, but not constrained; perplexed, but not driven to despair; persecuted, but not abandoned; struck down, but not destroyed; always carrying about in our bodies the dying of Jesus, so that the life of Jesus may also be manifested in our body." (2 Cor. 4:7-10)

Sometimes things look their worst, when God is doing his best. I recall a road sign that I have never forgotten: Temporary inconvenience for permanent improvement. God healed me from the inside out.

When God is allowing you to look foolish in the eyes of the world, it's very easy to fall into the hands of Mr. FuWD-fear, worry and doubt. When the bills need to be paid and there is no money, when your loved ones are sick and there seems to be no cure, when it looks like the world has gone to hell in a hand basket, ...In all things, at all times God is beckoning us to trust. St. Therese summarized her little childlike way, with these words, "It is to be disturbed by nothing." The minute you feel yourself beginning to worry, cry out "My Jesus I Trust in You." We need to have faith and trust greater than the Apostles when they were with Jesus on the Sea of Galilee and a storm came up, "A violent squall arose and waves were breaking over the boat, so that it was already filling up. Jesus was in the stern, asleep on a cushion. They woke him and said to him, "Teacher, do you not care that we are perishing?" He woke up, rebuked the wind, and said to the sea, "Quiet! Be still!" The wind ceased and there was great calm. Then he asked them, "Why are you terrified? Do you not yet have faith?" (Mark 4:37-40)

Jesus rebuked the wind but He also rebuked the apostles. Don't you think He could have shown a little more compassion? After all, the waves were huge, the boat was filled with water and He was just snoozing away. Well, He had just healed the lame, given sight to the blind and raised the widow's son in their presence. Now a storm rises up and they are in a panic.

How many times do we get like this? Do we not know that amidst life's storms, the One who is with us, even though He might seem asleep at the wheel, is the One who takes such joy in us and does not let anything happen to us that would separate us from Him. "For I am convinced that neither death, nor life, nor angels, nor principalities, nor present things, nor future things, nor powers, nor height, nor depth, nor any other creature will be able to separate us from the love of God in Christ Jesus our Lord." (Romans 9:38-39) Writing in the 16th century, St. Teresa of Avila echoed St. Paul's words, "Let nothing trouble you, let nothing frighten you, all is fleeting, God alone is unchanging. Patience obtains everything. Who possesses God wants for nothing. God alone suffices." She knew that the Lord was with her and she trusted in Him that He would take care of everything.

I find that I am most tempted to worry when I think I that the success or failure of whatever I am involved in depends on me. The Divine paradox is that we work like everything depends on us, pray as if everything depends on God and trust that whatever ultimately happens is God's perfect will.

As we abandon ourselves to Christ we will see that so often we can do all that appears to be "the right thing" and produce a bad result, and do nothing right and the produce the desired outcome. We find that God's power is greater than our lack of power and his function is greater than our dysfunction. Ultimately we find that "All is Grace."

God calls us to complete and total abandonment. It is when we "delight in the Lord" that He grants us our heart's desire."(Ps.37:4) This is where the supernatural indifference of the Saints comes from: joy or pain, consolation or dryness, light or darkness, adulation or criticism, honey or gall, health or sickness, life or death (I Believe in Love by Father Jean C.J. d"Elbee p.98); "It's all good" because it comes from our Father and "Father knows best."

Three years ago Paul and I felt the Lord calling us to leave Steubenville, Ohio. We felt like Abraham when he was told to back it up and move to the land of Ur. I had retired from my career as an advertising sales person and talk show host in order to be a full time domestic engineer. Because Paul had just graduated with his master's when we got married and I had been working for years, I was the primary breadwinner. When I was pregnant with our second child, Noah, I knew that it was God's will that I quit my job. I was completely confident that God would provide for us through Paul's work. After Noah's birth, we had a special presentation of him in the temple (Holy Family Church that is) in commemoration of the dedication of Jesus as an infant. That Monday, Paul lost his job. Blessed be Jesus; thank you for everything.

Paul got a job in Pennsylvania that promised to be very lucrative. We praised Jesus that He was taking us to the Promised Land. We prayed every step of the way and with signs and wonders found a townhouse to rent. It should not have been available but the person who was scheduled to lease it cancelled as we sat in the office. We weren't supposed to be able to get in to see it but after we finished the prayer," Lord, if it's Your will that we see inside before committing, please let us be able to get in, Amen"; and a woman came across the green and asked if we would like to see her place. Thank you Jesus.

Well, day turned into night and night turned into day and Paul's promising job never came through on the promise. My Mom kept asking me about Shirley: Shirley Paul didn't come in to the marriage with debt?, Shirley you have savings to sustain you? Shirley you have a plan…Shirley-you-are-perishing!!

I used to love to get friends and family beautiful gifts to show how much God and I loved them. I'd pray first and then get to see how God inspired just the right purchase at just the right time. Now I don't exchange gifts at all. I used to love to make gourmet dinners for my guests, shopping ahead so I could get the ingredients on sale. Now we can't shop ahead because there is no money after the rent is paid. At the feet of my parents, I learned that it's irresponsible and dangerous to let your gas tank run on empty and yet couldn't do it differently when I had to pick up my poor mother at the airport. She nearly had a heart attack when we sat in traffic as the empty gas tank alert buzzer sounded. Can you say "humilification?" That's my word for the humblings and mortifications that God permit to occur at the least opportune time. Yet, "God works all things together for good for those who love the Lord and are called according to his plan."(Romans 8:28)

God has used these times of trial to produce an abundant harvest. Let's go fruit picking for just a moment. He's given us the opportunity to experience the true meaning of "Give us this day our daily bread" and my family marvels at how Paul and I can be so joyful in the midst of our financial woes. We have many relatives who have "mucho dinero" but very little grace and unfortunately divorce has been the result. All of the sufferings related to our daily challenges are promptly offered up for the salvation of souls; we've grown in the faith that is the realization of things hoped for and the evidence of things unseen. (Hebrews 11:1)

The secret of holiness lies in union and communion with Love, Himself. It's always giving your beloved God the benefit of the doubt even when the answers to your prayers are not observable to the natural eye. St. Augustine relates in his "confessions" that when he lived in Carthage with his parents, he made the decision to go to Rome to teach. He wasn't a saint at the time. His mother, Monica, who wanted nothing more than the salvation of his soul, thought that this departure, which took him away from her influence in order to expose him to all the temptations of Rome, would be the end of all her hope.

He writes" Why I left one country and went to the other, you knew O God, but you did not tell me or my mother. She indeed was in dreadful grief and followed me to the seacoast. There she clung to me, passionately, determined that that I should either go back home with her or take her to Rome. I stole away while she remained in the Oratory of St. Cyprian praying and weeping. And what was she praying for, O my God, with all those tears but that I should not sail! But you saw deeper and granted the essential part of her prayer: You did not do what she was at that moment asking, that you might do the thing she was always asking.

St. Monica was opposed to his departure, but it was in Italy that Augustine was to encounter St. Ambrose, who was an instrument of his conversion. (I Believe in love-pp.101-102)

When I'm homeschooling, I often have to challenge my children to focus, focus, focus; "For without a vision the people perish." Half of what we experience is how we look at it. When we see everything as from the hands of our loving Father "who knows the plans he has in store for us - for a future full of hope and not of woe," we are encouraged. As I mentioned before, we live in a townhouse complex. In between the parking lot and our front door is a vast expanse of green grass. It's an absolute gift to find such a large, safe lawn for the children to play on. I can let them outside while I'm cooking dinner without fearing for their precious lives. All the neighborhood children can ride their bicycles safely on the huge sidewalks that line the building. However, It can take a half hour to mobilize the troops, pack up the stroller, buckle them all in, only to realize you forgot something back at the ranch. Upon returning from wherever, it's a really long walk from the parking lot in the snow, sleet and rain with 10 bags of groceries and two sleeping children. Both descriptions are accurate; both are opportunities to praise God. The first is self-evident. The second because, on a good day, I can embrace the opportunity to offer up the inconvenience as a prayer for souls; or I can grumble and make everyone miserable recalling that our humble abode is located on Egypt Road where the phone exchange is 666. What were we thinking?

Looking Heavenward, I have been a Catholic now for 18 years (which means life in Hebrew), I just turned 40 and I have a son named Moses. All these can be seen as evidence that the odds are in my favor. Even as I am offering up our flight into Egypt, I'm faithfully awaiting deliverance to our new life in the Promised Land (with a house, a garage and our own backyard). Never the less, Thy will be done.

Holiness is not about doing what we want but it is about doing what he wants us to do in love and for love. St. Therese, the Little Flower wanted to be a missionary to make Love loved. But instead of sending her out into the mission fields, God called her to be hidden in a four-walled enclosure.

We are called to love God by giving Him ourselves in total surrender uniting our will to His. He longs for us to rest confidently on his breast, believing in the love He has for us and rejoicing even in our weaknesses. Little Therese understood that "it is our state of misery which attracts His mercy." St. Paul wrote, "Gladly, therefore I will glory in my infirmities, that the power of Christ may dwell in me." (2 Cor. 12:9)

I shared earlier, that I gave up my career in advertising, like Abraham when he offered up Isaac. God gave it back to me for a time, until I retired to be at home with the children. I have come face to face with my powerlessness in this forum as never before.

In the work world, there is at least an illusion of mastery and accomplishment. You have your little Day Timer, you plan your plan and you execute it. You may have obstacles to overcome but they don't overcome you. In the land of the little people, you can plan the plans but the only sure thing is that it won't turn out as planned. The curtain is up before you know your lines and your riding on a wing and a prayer. As many times as I have said, "I will not negotiate with terrorists (my high energy, strong-willed 4 year old, 100% boy), I find myself saying, "Drop the gun, Noah, Drop the gun!" I call my little Moses, my Visa card because he's everywhere you want to be; His goodnight lullaby is "Ain't no mountain high enough" because there ain't nothing he can't climb.

I had no illusions about my abilities as a domestic goddess-I was just praying for the grace to make it through the day and then God began to ask more of me. I knew that I knew that I knew that God was calling me to homeschool but I fought it tooth and nail. Then He inspired the creation of "Seraphim Cakes-a Taste of Heaven" my home-based gourmet cake business and opened up the door for a career in Real Estate. (Now I can get you a Taste of Heaven and a Piece of Earth). To top it off, He opened the door to numerous speaking engagements. I'd pray, and I'd hear and see all around me the phrase "I can do all things through Christ who strengthens me." O.K., Lord, but do you want me to do all things???

St. Therese wanted to be a missionary and instead was confined to the 4 walls of the convent. I was content to be hidden in the heart of my home and God has me brought me here, there and everywhere.

The path to Holiness is an incredible journey we make carried on the wings of God's love. It's the day in, day out, awful and awesome, stupid and stupendous things in our lives that God uses to perfect us. It is in the midst of the mess that He will make us holy, not in spite of it. Face it, we are all going to suffer, the question is; "Will it be redemptive, will it produce the fruit of holiness within us." Holiness is a by-product of living your life for God. Do his will, embrace your daily crosses and He will do all the rest within you, making you into the Saint that He calls you to be. The words of St. Paul will become your own, "For his sake I have accepted the loss of all things and I consider them rubbish, that I may gain Christ...to know him and the power of his resurrection and the sharing of his sufferings by being conformed to his death, if somehow I may attain the resurrection from the dead." (Phil 3:8-11)

Since that time God has carried me through many a trial. Like St. Paul said in Phil 4:12 I can truly say: "I know what it is like to have little and what it is like to have plenty. In any and all circumstances I have learned the secret of being well fed and of going hungry, of having plenty and of being in need. I have strength for everything through him who empowers me."

I have suffered the loss of 6 babies: Celine, Joseph, Maria, Matthew, John and James. I was blessed to have had the opportunity to baptize most of them. When we found out that Joseph's heart had stopped beating, the doctors told me that I needed to have a D and C.

I refused because I wanted the chance to baptize him if I could. I know that God would take care and receive our precious little one if I didn't but if I could do it I wanted to. The doctors said that I wouldn't even be able to recognize him as a baby. I waited until he came out naturally 3 weeks later. HE WAS TOTALLY RECOGNIZABLE. HE DIED AT 10 1/2 WEEKS AND YOU COULD SEE HIS PERFECTLY FORMED TOES AND FINGERS. HE EVEN HAD A SMILE ON HIS FACE. See his picture on the next page.

We had a funeral service for him which we opened up to all our friends who had suffered the loss of a baby and it was truly a healing balm to everyone. We sang the song 'Blessed be the Name of the Lord'; you give and take away, still my heart will choose to say, Lord blessed be your name. We gave a picture of little Joseph to a friend who gave it to a girl who was contemplating an abortion and little Joseph turned her heart around. He keeps interceding for the unborn as our champion for life. "For we know that God works all things together for good for those who love the Lord and are called according to his plan." Romans 8:28

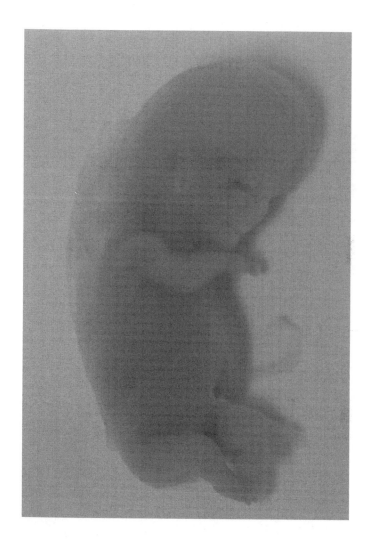

Joseph Michael Burdett

10.5 weeks in utero

died 1/25/06

born/baptized 2/12/06

buried 2/18/06

Cindy is available to present her conversion story to groups or parishes, contact her at 484-802-8982 or via email at CindyBurdett@yahoo.com for speaking availability and fees.

Made in the USA
Middletown, DE
16 April 2024

53105433R00028